Dear Parent:
Your child's love of reading starts here!

Every child learns to read in a different way and at his or her own speed. Some go back and forth between reading levels and read favorite books again and again. Others read through each level in order. You can help your young reader improve and become more confident by encouraging his or her own interests and abilities. From books your child reads with you to the first books he or she reads alone, there are I Can Read Books for every stage of reading:

SHARED READING
Basic language, word repetition, and whimsical illustrations, ideal for sharing with your emergent reader

1
BEGINNING READING
Short sentences, familiar words, and simple concepts for children eager to read on their own

2
READING WITH HELP
Engaging stories, longer sentences, and language play for developing readers

3
READING ALONE
Complex plots, challenging vocabulary, and high-interest topics for the independent reader

I Can Read Books have introduced children to the joy of reading since 1957. Featuring award-winning authors and illustrators and a fabulous cast of beloved characters, I Can Read Books set the standard for beginning readers.

A lifetime of discovery begins with the magical words **"I Can Read!"**

Visit www.icanread.com for information
on enriching your child's reading experience.

Cyn—strong women are never forgotten
—*K. D. & S. R. J.*

For my amazing friend Aly.
Thank you for everything <3
—*J. M.*

The full-color artwork was created digitally.

I Can Read® and I Can Read Book® are trademarks of HarperCollins Publishers.

Vivi Loves Science: Wind and Water. Text copyright © 2023 by Kimberly Derting and Shelli R. Johannes. Illustrations copyright © 2023 by Joelle Murray. All rights reserved. No part of this book may be used or reproduced in any manner whatsoever without written permission except in the case of brief quotations embodied in critical articles and reviews. Printed in the USA. For information address HarperCollins Children's Books, a division of HarperCollins Publishers, 195 Broadway, New York, NY 10007. www.icanread.com

Library of Congress Control Number: 2022947260
ISBN 978-0-06-311660-3 (hardcover) — ISBN 978-0-06-311659-7 (paperback)

23 24 25 26 27   CWM   10 9 8 7 6 5 4 3 2   ❖   First Edition
Greenwillow Books

I Can Read!

Vivi

LOVES SCIENCE

Wind and Water

By KIMBERLY DERTING
and SHELLI R. JOHANNES
pictures by JOELLE MURRAY

Greenwillow Books
An Imprint of HarperCollins Publishers

Vivi listened to the wind howl.
She watched the rain splash against
her window.
It was a stormy night, but Vivi felt safe
and warm tucked in her bed.

"Did you hear the storm last night?"
Vivi asked at breakfast the next morning.
"Yes!" said Vivi's mother. "It was a big one."

"I heard Ranger Earle needs volunteers to help clean up the beach," said Vivi's father. "Let's go!" Vivi jumped up from the table. "Graeme can come too!"

When Vivi and Graeme got to the beach, they couldn't believe what they saw.

There were bottles covering the dunes.

There were cans on the sand.

And there was debris everywhere.

The beach was a mess.

It also looked completely different.

"Where are the tide pools?" asked Vivi.

"What happened to the dunes?" asked Graeme.

"A big storm can change the shape
of the land," Ranger Earle explained.

"But how?" Vivi asked.

"Storms can cause erosion," said Ranger Earle.
"What is erosion?" asked Vivi.

"Erosion is when natural forces, such as wind
or water, move or wear away rock or soil,"
Ranger Earle said. "Erosion can change
a coastline and create rivers and canyons."

"Wow!" said Vivi. "Like the Grand Canyon?"

"That's right!" said Ranger Earle.

Vivi and Graeme took a break to have a snack.

Ranger Earle told them about other famous examples of erosion from around the world.

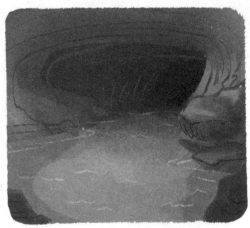

Mammoth Cave

White Cliffs of Dover

Elephant Trunk Hill

"Erosion can happen very quickly, like with this big storm," she said. "Or it can take a very long time, even millions of years."

Ms. Cousteau, Vivi and Graeme's science
teacher at school, was helping to clean up
the beach, too.

"Hi, kids!" said Ms. Cousteau.

"Did you know that the storm filled in
the tide pools?" Vivi asked her.

"Ranger Earle told us how wind and water can change the shape of the land," Graeme said. "Look at the new dunes!"

"They were caused by erosion!" said Vivi.

"You got it!" said Ms. Cousteau. "Ocean waves are a powerful force, and so is the wind."

Graeme and
Vivi worked
hard to clean up
the beach.
They picked up
the bottles.

They hauled
away
the cans.

And they collected
the garbage.
It took all day.

Luckily, many people from their community
pitched in and helped.

The next day in science class, Vivi and Graeme told their friends about how the beach had changed because of the storm.

"Yesterday, Graeme and Vivi learned about erosion," Ms. Cousteau said.
"Today, they will do an experiment to show us how wind and water can move sand."

Ms. Cousteau gave everyone a worksheet. She gave Vivi and Graeme the materials for the experiment.

They had two containers,

sand,

water,

and

a straw.

"Earth science is the study of how the earth changes over time," Ms. Cousteau said. "Wind and water are important forces on Earth."

Graeme dumped sand into one container, making a small hill.

"First, we will talk about water," he said.

"Did you know that water erosion creates rivers and streams?" Vivi asked.

"Water can also carve out caves and hills and make cracks in the rocks," Graeme added.

Vivi picked up a container of water. "Watch what happens when I pour water on the sand. I'm pretending to be the rain," she said.

"See how the water ran down the hill?"
Graeme said. "It pushed the sand
out of the way and made
a river."

"That's erosion!" Vivi exclaimed.
"That's so cool," said Mia.

Graeme dumped a pile of sand into the other container.

"Now, we will talk about wind," he said.

"Did you know that wind helps make sand dunes at the beach?" Vivi asked.

"And some sand dunes in the desert are thousands of feet high," Graeme added.

"Taller than the tallest buildings in the world!" Vivi said.

This time, Vivi used the straw.

She blew on the sand.

"I am pretending to be the wind," she said.

"See how the wind moved the sand?"
Graeme said.

"Look." Mia pointed. "The pile of sand
changed shape."

"I think erosion is cool!" Benji said.

"It is! But sometimes erosion can be dangerous," said Ms. Cousteau.

"For example, sand dunes are important because they keep water from traveling inland and flooding towns and homes."

"I bet that's why we can't walk on the dunes," Vivi said.

Ms. Cousteau nodded. "That's right. We don't want to crush the plants that hold the sand dunes together."

On Saturday, Vivi and Graeme went back to the beach.

"Look! The tide pools are here!" said Vivi.

"Good point. The wind and waves from the storm moved the sand in," Ranger Earle said. "And the water from the tide took the sand away again."

"Without erosion, we wouldn't have the beach," Graeme said.

Vivi smiled. "Without science," she said, "we wouldn't know how things work. Science is the best!"

Vivi

LOVES SCIENCE

Erosion Experiment

Erosion occurs when the earth's surface is worn away by wind, water, or ice. This experiment takes a closer look at wind and water erosion.

Materials

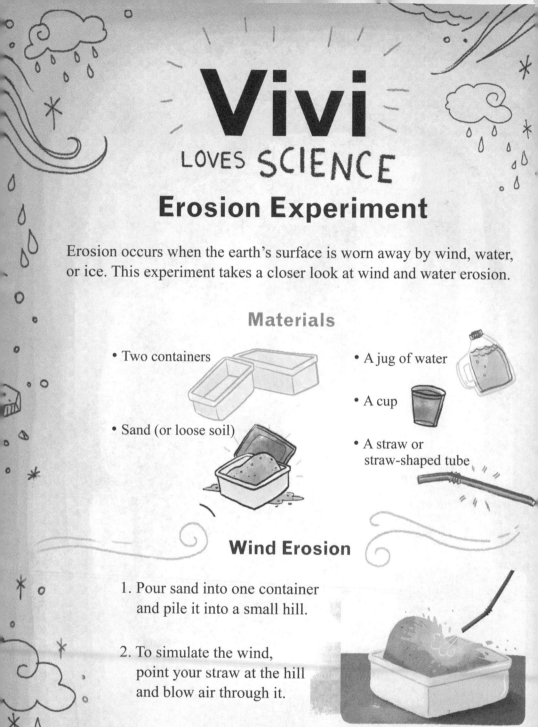

- Two containers

- Sand (or loose soil)

- A jug of water

- A cup

- A straw or straw-shaped tube

Wind Erosion

1. Pour sand into one container and pile it into a small hill.

2. To simulate the wind, point your straw at the hill and blow air through it.

What happened to the hill? What effect did the wind have on the hill?

3. Now, flatten the hill and try the experiment again.

Did the sand move as much when the ground was flat?

4. Rebuild the hill and try adding rocks or plants and then blowing again.

What happened? Did you get just as much erosion as before?

 **Water Erosion**

1. Pour sand into one container and pile it into a small hill.

2. To simulate the rain, pour water onto the top of your mountain.

What happened to the hill? What effect did the water have on the sand?

Try adding rocks or other objects to see if they change, or slow, the pattern of erosion.

What happened? Did you get as much erosion as before?

Having fun with **Wind** and **Water**
What created these places on Earth?
Wind, water, or both?

A valley

Wind or water?

Dunes

Wind or water?

Caves

Wind or water?

Canyon

Wind or water?

Glossary

Deposition: When the material that has eroded is deposited in a new area.

Earth science: The study of the planet Earth, including its weather.

Erosion: The wearing away of land by water, wind, and even ice.

Water: The liquid that forms the oceans, lakes, rivers, and rain.

Wind: A current of air that moves across the earth's surface.